GEORGE ARMSTRONG

CusteR

A BIOGRAPHY

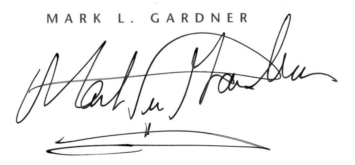

For Welda & Richard Fosry
with the warm best wishes
of their friend —

MARK L. GARDNER

WESTERN NATIONAL PARKS ASSOCIATION

TUCSON, ARIZONA

Published by Western National Parks Association
The net proceeds from WNPA publications support educational and research
programs in the national parks.
Receive a free Western National Parks Association catalog, featuring hundreds
of publications.
Email: info@wnpa.org or visit www.wnpa.org

WRITTEN BY Mark L. Gardner

EDITED BY Derek Gallagher

DESIGNED BY Nancy Campana, Campana Design

PHOTOGRAPHY BY: *Front cover*: Little Bighorn Battlefield National Monument. *Pages 3
and 4*: Little Bighorn Battlefield National Monument. *Page 6*: Jeff Gnass. *Page 8*: Little
Bighorn Battlefield National Monument. *Page 11*: Getty Images. *Page 12*: Jeff Gnass.
Pages 16-17: Little Bighorn Battlefield National Monument. *Page 18*: Fred Hirschmann.
Page 23: Little Bighorn Battlefield National Monument. *Page 24*: Little Bighorn
Battlefield National Monument. *Page 28*: Steve Mulligan. *Page 30*: Tom Bean. *Page 34*:
Little Bighorn Battlefield National Monument. *Page 36*: J. C. Leacock. *Pages 38 and 41*:
Tom Bean. *Page 42*: Jeff Gnass. *Pages 44 and 45*: Little Bighorn Battlefield National
Monument. *Page 48*: Denver Public Library, Western History Collection, Call No. X-
33630.

PRINTING BY Everbest Printing Co. through Four Colour Imports, Ltd.

PRINTED IN China

CONTENTS

*If there was any
poetry or romance in war he could develop it.*

MAJ. GEN. PHILIP SHERIDAN,
REMEMBERING CUSTER

Washington, D.C., May 23, 1865. Thousands of crowding spectators thrill to the sight of columns upon columns of Union soldiers marching through the streets of the nation's capital. It is the "Grand Review," an immense parade celebrating the end of four years of bitter warfare between North and South. At the head of his famed cavalry division rides Brevet Major General George Armstrong Custer on a steed known as Don Juan. As they near the gaily decorated review stand of President Andrew Johnson, Custer's horse suddenly becomes frightened when a group of girls burst into song and throw numerous wreaths and bouquets at the general. Custer and Don Juan race headlong down Pennsylvania Avenue, Custer managing a salute as he passes before the president's review stand. Then "by one of the most magnificent exhibitions of horsemanship he in a moment reined in the flying charger, and returned to meet his troops," recalled an observer. It is the most breathtaking scene of the two-day parade and a fitting capstone to Custer's illustrious Civil War career.

Just nine years earlier, Custer had been a teenaged schoolteacher in Ohio, earning a salary of $28 a month. And just eleven years after that wild glorious ride with Don Juan he would lie stripped and dead on a grassy hillside overlooking the valley of the Little Bighorn River in present-day Montana.

MARBLE MARKER AT LITTLE BIGHORN BATTLEFIELD NATIONAL MONUMENT SHOWING WHERE CUSTER WAS INITIALLY BURIED.

THE LIFE AND TIMES OF

George Armstrong Custer

DECEMBER 9, 1839	Born at New Rumley, Ohio.
1857	Admitted to the U.S. Military Academy at West Point.
JUNE 26, 1863	Appointed Brigadier General of U.S. Volunteers.
FEBRUARY 9, 1864	Marries Elizabeth "Libbie" Bacon of Monroe, Michigan.
APRIL 8–9, 1865	Custer's division captures Lee's supplies at Appomattox and blocks his escape route. Custer receives flag of truce signaling the end of the war.
1866	Accepts lieutenant-colonelcy of the newly formed Seventh Cavalry at Fort Riley, Kansas.
1867	Takes part in the Hancock Expedition against the Plains Indians. Court-martialed for absence without leave from his command and the unmerciful treatment of deserters.
NOVEMBER 27, 1868	Attacks and destroys the Cheyenne village of Black Kettle in what becomes known as the Battle of the Washita.
1872	Participates in the Grand Duke Alexis's widely publicized hunting party on the Plains.
1873	Custer and the Seventh escort Northern Pacific Railroad engineers as part of the Yellowstone Expedition.
1874	Commands the Black Hills Expedition—reports discovery of gold. Custer publishes book: *My Life on the Plains*.
JUNE 25, 1876	Is Killed with more than 200 of his men at the Battle of the Little Bighorn, Montana.

CADET CUSTER AT AGE 21

AUTIE

You and I are going home today,
and by a trail that is strange to us both.

HALF-YELLOW-FACE, CROW SCOUT,
TO CUSTER, JUNE 25, 1876

George Armstrong Custer was born to Emanuel Henry and Maria Ward Kirkpatrick Custer at New Rumley, Ohio, on December 5, 1839. Emanuel, a skilled blacksmith, and Maria had each lost a spouse before their 1836 marriage and each brought children to the union, but George was their first child together to survive infancy, and he is said to have been a favored son for that reason. The Custer family would grow even larger in the years to come with the addition of siblings Nevin, Thomas Ward, Boston, and Margaret. George, initially called Armstrong by his proud parents, quickly picked up the nickname "Autie," from the way he first pronounced his own middle name.

As a young boy, George no doubt helped his father in his busy smithy, a perfect place to learn about both people and horse-flesh. When George was ten, his father sold the blacksmith shop in town and moved the family to a nearby farm. About this same time, George went to live with his older stepsister, Lydia Ann, and her husband David Reed in Monroe, Michigan. Lydia had helped her mother raise young George, and the two were very close. In Monroe, George attended first the New Dublin School and then Stebbin's Academy for Boys. One of his classmates at the Stebbin's school remembered George's love of military novels and how the young scholar would hide an open copy of *Charles O'Malley, the Irish Dragoon* (1841) beneath his open geography book and quickly pretend to be tracing some geographical feature when Schoolmaster Stebbin passed by Custer's desk. Stebbin would "pat the boy's head and pronounce him a credit to the school, a compliment received by the youngster with an edifying air of virtuous humility."

The youthful Custer's interest in things military was not unusual. The same could be said for just about every boy of antebellum America, whose heroes were military figures like George Washington, Andrew Jackson, and Zachary Taylor. A favorite story was often told of how Emanuel Custer would take his four-year-old son with him to the local militia musters in New Rumley. Autie, wearing a miniature uniform made by his mother, would delight the militia members by going through the manual of arms with his toy musket.

In 1855 Custer was back in Ohio attending a boarding school, and later that year he accepted a teaching position at a school in Athens Township — he was just fifteen years old. He somehow found time to continue his own education and in 1856 acquired a teacher's certificate. He accepted another teaching position in Cadiz Township that summer, but by now Custer had set his sights on the United States Military Academy at West Point. He was well aware that a West Point education offered a young man of limited means an opportunity to better his situation, and if a war should break out in which one could win laurels, so much the better.

Thus, Custer began a correspondence with Congressman John W. Bingham of Ohio to obtain an appointment to the Academy. In one letter, Custer related that he was "above the medium height and of remarkably strong constitution and vigorous frame." Custer actually stood five feet nine and three-fourths inches tall. One of his Civil War subordinates later remembered him as "tall, lithe, active, muscular, straight as an Indian and as quick in his movements…[with] the fair complexion of a school girl." Custer got his appointment to West Point in 1857.

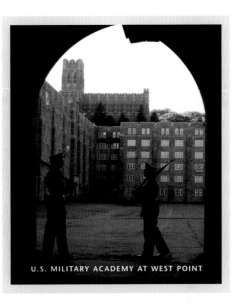

U.S. MILITARY ACADEMY AT WEST POINT

Much has been written of Custer's time at West Point, his unending pranks, poor grades, and countless infractions (his four-year total of demerits came to 726). His rebellious nature no doubt partly explains his universal popularity with the other cadets. Custer admitted in later years, though, "My career as a cadet had but little to commend it to the study of those who came after me, unless as an example to be carefully avoided." In short, George Armstrong Custer just scraped by at the Academy, graduating 34th in a class of 34. Yet Custer's class originally numbered 68 individuals in 1857. To graduate from West Point, whether at the top or bottom of one's class, was a significant achievement. Custer would always recall his days at West Point with fondness and would later express a wish to be buried in the Academy's cemetery.

COLD HARBOR BATTLEFIELD AT
RICHMOND NATIONAL BATTLEFIELD
PARK IN VIRGINIA

BROTHER
AGAINST BROTHER

It is useless to hope the coming struggle will be bloodless
or of short duration. Much blood will be spilled and
thousands of lives, at the least, lost.

CUSTER TO LYDIA ANN REED, 1861

One of Custer's vivid recollections of his cadet years was of the division that soon developed between his brothers from Northern and Southern states. Slavery was a topic of heated discussion, as was the presidential election of 1860. Custer remembered one night when Republican candidate Abraham Lincoln was hung in effigy from a tree in front of the cadet barracks. The Southern states promised to secede if Lincoln won the election, and the Southern cadets declared they would leave the Academy when their states left the Union.

"You cannot imagine how sorry I will be to see this happen," Custer wrote his stepsister Lydia Ann, "as the majority of my best friends and all my roommates except one have been from the South."

Custer graduated with his classmates on June 24, 1861. Almost a month later, as a brand new second lieutenant in the Second U.S. Cavalry, Custer got to see the Union army whipped at the Battle of Bull Run. He wrote that he little imagined he would be returning to Washington, D.C., with "a defeated and demoralized army." As the Northern leaders regrouped, Custer trained volunteer recruits at the outer defenses of Washington and served variously as an aide on the staffs of three different generals. That fall he returned to his stepsister's home in Monroe on sick leave. While there he engaged in a now-legendary drinking spree with an old friend, the embarrassing effects of which led him to vow never again to partake of ardent spirits. It was a vow, so far as we know, that he never broke.

The spring of 1862 found Custer attached to the staff of Gen. William F. "Baldy" Smith during the ill-fated Peninsular Campaign against Richmond. His first assignment under Smith was to ascend in one of Thaddeus Lowe's hydrogen gas balloons and observe Confederate activity at the Union siege of Yorktown, Virginia. Custer performed this duty well, but he yearned for real combat on the ground, and whenever it came, Custer could invariably be found, as he once wrote, "in the thick of the fight." During the Battle of Williamsburg on May 5, Custer, on his own initiative, galloped forward and led an infantry charge that won the day for the North. The plucky lieutenant single-handedly captured a rebel captain and five men along with a Confederate battle flag. This flag was the first seized by the Army of the Potomac.

Custer skirmished again with the Rebs on May 24. He had previously waded the Chickahominy River into enemy territory and observed a Confederate outpost near New Bridge. Leading members of Companies A and B of the Fourth Michigan Infantry (which were composed of men from Custer's old home of

Monroe), the lieutenant again crossed the river and proceeded downstream to attack the rebel position. Simultaneously, the remainder of the Michigan regiment moved parallel to Custer on the opposite side of the Chickahominy. Custer's surprise attack overran the rebel outpost and continued to their nearby camp. Custer grabbed a large bowie knife from a Confederate prisoner and splashed his horse across the river to lend encouragement to the rest of the Michiganders. Swinging the bowie above his head, Custer roared, "The Rebels say we can't stand cold steel. I captured this from one of them. Forward and show them that the Michigan boys will give them all the cold steel they want."

Custer's actions on the Chickahominy were brought to the attention of Maj. Gen. George B. McClellan, commander of the Army of the Potomac, who sent for the young man to thank him. McClellan offered Custer a position on his personal staff as aide-de-camp, which Custer gladly accepted. The position carried the temporary rank of captain. "In those days," McClellan wrote in his memoirs, "Custer was simply a reckless, gallant boy, undeterred by fatigue, unconscious of fear; and he always brought me clear and intelligible reports of what he saw when under the heaviest fire. I became much attached to him."

Custer idolized McClellan, but his commander's dismal performance during the Peninsular Campaign and failure to take the offensive after the Battle of Antietam signaled the end of McClellan's military career. In November Custer traveled on leave to Monroe. At a Thanksgiving party he was formally introduced to a young woman of a prominent local family named Elizabeth Bacon. Her relatives and friends called her Libbie. "When I think how in those few minutes you could have made up your mind about me," Libbie later wrote Custer, "and how you made the only impression that went below the surface of my seemingly impressionable heart it is a miracle."

GEN. PHILIP SHERIDAN AND STAFF IN JANUARY 1865. FROM LEFT, GEN. WESLEY MERRITT, GEN. PHILIP SHERIDAN, GEN. GEORGE CROOK, GEN. WILLIAM FORSYTH, AND GEN. GEORGE CUSTER.

CANNON ON SEMINARY RIDGE,
GETTYSBURG NATIONAL MILITARY
PARK, PENNSYLVANIA

Boy General

So brave a man I never saw and as competent as brave. Under him a man is ashamed to be cowardly. Under him our men can achieve wonders.

MAJ. JAMES HENRY KIDD,
6TH MICHIGAN CAVALRY, JUNE 3, 1864

Custer rejoined the Army of the Potomac in May 1863, just a few days after the federal defeat at the Battle of Chancellorsville. Custer was again on staff duty, this time with Brig. Gen. Alfred Pleasonton. Pleasonton had advocated the consolidation of the federal cavalry, which had previously been used piecemeal, into a single fighting corps. This reorganization occurred early in 1863, with Pleasonton receiving the cavalry command shortly after Custer joined his staff. Custer repeatedly distinguished himself on the battlefield, quickly gaining the admiration and friendship of Pleasonton.

The general came to trust his aide so much that he left many battlefield decisions to Custer. An orderly recalled that if Custer determined it was necessary to change a position or make a charge, he would tell the immediate commanding officer to do it, and that officer "would not dare question, because he knew . . . Custer was working under General Pleasonton who would confirm every one of his instructions and movements."

In late June, as Gen. Robert E. Lee's invading Army of Northern Virginia marched into Pennsylvania, the federal cavalry corps underwent another reorganization. Pleasonton requested the appointment of three brigadier generals to serve under him. One of the three he requested was Brevet Captain Custer (a brevet was an honorary rank). The promotion became official on June 29—Custer was just 23 years old. "To say I was elated," Custer wrote a friend, "would faintly express my feelings." To his stepsister Lydia Ann he declared, "I am the youngest General in the U.S. Army by over two years, in itself something to be proud of." Custer may have been surprised and proud, but there were other officers who were dismayed and jealous. Such a jump in rank was simply unheard of.

Custer took charge of the Second Brigade, Third Division, which he dubbed the Wolverines, as the brigade was made up entirely of Michigan cavalry regiments. Now that he was a general with his own command, Custer could give free rein to the romantic notions of war and chivalry he had thrilled to in his childhood. He put together his own uniform of navy blue velvet, the sleeves of which he had covered with elaborate gold lace. The oversized lapels of a blue "navy shirt" flapped over the top of his jacket, and to this he added a dapper crimson necktie. Atop his head, at a rakish angle, sat a black wide-brimmed hat adorned by a single silver star. "His golden hair fell in graceful luxuriance nearly or quite to his shoulders," wrote one of Custer's officers, "and his upper lip was garnished with a blond mustache. A sword and belt, gilt spurs and top boots completed his unique outfit." One less-than-charitable observer thought Custer looked like "a circus rider gone mad!"

At the Battle of Gettysburg on July 3, Custer's Wolverines went up against the cavalry of the legendary Confederate Maj. Gen. J.E.B. Stuart and played an instrumental role in his defeat. Before the month of July was out, Custer had had three horses shot out from under him—he would lose more in the months to come. But the "Boy General," as he was sometimes called in the newspapers, was not simply exposing himself through personal heroics. He was becoming a master in the use of cavalry in combat. "The only way to succeed in cavalry is to work quickly," wrote one of Custer's Wolverines, "the more like lightning, the better, for this is the true mode of mounted fighting; this was the secret of many of Custer's victories." This was no secret to the best cavalry commanders, though, including Custer's opponent Stuart, who declared that "an attack of cavalry should be sudden, bold, and vigorous." Such maxims would still pertain when Custer engaged the Cheyenne and Lakota at the Little Bighorn in 1876.

Custer received thirty days' leave in January 1864 to wed Libbie Bacon in Monroe. The ceremony took place at the First Presbyterian Church (the building still stands) on February 9, after which the newlyweds traveled to West Point and New York City. Custer and his Wolverines were back in action by the end of the month, and in March, Maj. Gen. Philip H. Sheridan, or "Little Phil," replaced Pleasonton as head of the Cavalry Corps. Sheridan took 10,000 troopers on a raid toward Richmond that May. The Second Brigade gathered additional laurels at places called Yellow Tavern (where a Wolverine mortally wounded J.E.B. Stuart), Haw's Shop, and Trevilian Station (where Custer and his Wolverines were surrounded and held at bay for three hours).

In August, Sheridan began operations in the Shenandoah Valley, the "breadbasket of the Confederacy." At the Battle of Winchester on September 19, Custer with 500 men routed 1,600 entrenched Confederate infantrymen, taking 700 prisoners and seven battle flags. Two months later, having earned the command of the Third Cavalry Division, Custer struck a decisive blow against Jubal Early's army at the Battle of Cedar Creek, capturing forty-five cannon, five flags, and even more prisoners. A few days later, standing before Secretary of War Edwin Stanton with some of the trophies from Cedar Creek, Custer learned that he had been promoted (on Sheridan's recommendation) to brevet major general of volunteers. "General," Stanton addressed him, "a gallant officer always makes gallant soldiers."

The bitter end for the Confederate States of America came in March and April of 1865. Desperately short of supplies and with his defensive lines collapsing under the constant assaults of Ulysses S. Grant's forces, General Lee abandoned Richmond in hopes of linking up with another Rebel army in the Carolinas. At Appomattox Station on April 8, Custer's division pounced upon three trains filled with precious stores for Lee's famished soldiers and blocked the Rebel leader's escape route. The war all but ended the following day when Lee signed surrender terms written by Grant on a small table in the home of Wilmer McLean. The famous oval surrender table, now at the Smithsonian Institution, became the property of Phil Sheridan for the price of two $10 gold pieces. Little Phil in turn gave the table to Custer for his wife, Libbie. In a note to the proud Mrs. Custer, Sheridan wrote that "there is scarcely an individual in our service who has contributed more to bring about this desirable result than your gallant husband."

e~

ELIZABETH AND GEORGE CUSTER LESS THAN A
WEEK AFTER THEIR WEDDING IN FEBRUARY 1864

CUSTER WITH INDIAN SCOUTS DURING THE BLACK HILLS EXPEDITION IN 1874. BLOODY KNIFE, AN ARIKIRA SCOUT WHO ALSO DIED AT LITTLE BIGHORN BATTLEFIELD, POINTS AT THE MAP.

TO THE PLAINS
WITH THE SEVENTH U.S.
CAVALRY

[T]he 7th Cavalry . . .
as I am told by Genl. Hunter, and officers of the
War Department, is to be the finest regiment in the
service, and 'far superior to any of the old regiments.'

CAPT. ALBERT BARNITZ, JANUARY 17, 1867

Shortly after the Grand Review in Washington D.C., Custer, now a full major general of volunteers, was assigned by Sheridan to command a volunteer cavalry division in Texas. Custer and Libbie would remain in Texas only until February 1866. It was during this Texas sojourn, however, that the first sharply unsympathetic portraits of Custer began to appear. His men had generally idolized him during the glory days of the Civil War, but now the war was over, and the volunteers under his new command were anxious to go home. Desertion became rampant. Custer ultimately responded by ordering captured deserters to be flogged and their heads shaved. In at least one case, he had a deserter shot. The men branded Custer disloyal, inhuman, and tyrannical. In short, most hated the twenty six-year-old Boy General.

Custer's commission as a major general in the volunteer service expired at the end of December 1865, and he reverted to his last official rank in the regular army, that of captain in the Fifth U.S. Cavalry. Out of courtesy, however, people would continue to address Custer by the highest rank he had acheived during his Civil War service, a universal custom in the military. That March and April, Custer visited Washington, D.C., and New York City, all the while trying to decide his future. He was tempted by the idea of an appointment as a foreign minister; it paid "a salary in gold of from 7 to 10 thousand dollars per annum," he wrote Libbie.

The possibility of making good money also led Custer to consider seriously an offer to join the Mexican forces of President Benito Juárez in their fight to overthrow Archduke Ferdinand Maximilian, then ruling Mexico through the machinations of Napoleon III of France. Custer was offered the position of the Mexican army's adjutant general, for which services he would receive $10,000 in gold. But Custer failed to obtain the requisite year's leave of absence, leaving him no choice but to resign his commission to take the job, something Custer did not yet care to do.

The Army's creation of four additional cavalry regiments in 1866 offered Custer a temporary solution to his quandary. He accepted the lieutenant colonelcy of the new Seventh Cavalry, a unit intended to help protect the western plains. As a lieutenant colonel, Custer would officially be second in command of the regiment, but as the Seventh's colonel would seldom accompany the regiment in the field, the command—and any acclaim—would fall to Custer. Before departing for his new command, however, Custer agreed to travel with President Andrew Johnson and other dignitaries on a political tour around the country to drum up support for the president's reconstruction policy. Politicians would always court the famous Boy General, and he was not above using them to further his own career. Johnson's tour, despite the presence of heroes Custer and Grant, failed miserably.

By the time Custer arrived at Fort Riley, Kansas, the Seventh Cavalry's headquarters, much of the new regiment had been mustered in. More than a third of the troopers were immigrants from Ireland, Germany, and Great Britain. In civilian life, the men had been clerks, blacksmiths, porters, farmers, and laborers. And they were largely unprepared for the harsh realities of frontier service: hard campaigning, strict discipline, and isolation from loved ones. Custer and his officers would face some of the same challenges Custer had encountered in Texas, not the least of which was desertion. Eighty men deserted the Seventh by the end of 1866— the regiment had been in existence only five months! The first real test of the officers and men, though, came the following year.

For the most part, the troubles on the Plains had really started with the discovery of gold in Colorado in 1858. Boomtowns sprang up on Indian land; tremendous traffic—people, freight, and mail—passed through traditional bison-hunting grounds of the Cheyenne, Arapaho, and Lakota, and contact between whites and Plains dwellers became more frequent and often violent. The federal government entered into new treaties to remove the indigenous people from the proximity of the settlements and the overland trails, but while some Plains leaders signed the white man's paper, others vowed never to give up their homelands or their freedom. On November 29, 1864, Colorado volunteer troopers attacked the Cheyenne and Arapaho village of Chief Black Kettle, a village that had been promised safety by territorial and military officials. More than 160 Cheyenne, mostly women and children, were killed in what became known as the Sand Creek Massacre.

Following Sand Creek, there was renewed warfare, another treaty, and a period of relative peace on the central Plains. Then, in the spring of 1867, Maj. Gen. Winfield Scott Hancock led a large military expedition, including Custer and the Seventh Cavalry, onto the central Plains with the overall purpose of awing the Plains tribes. After holding a council with several chiefs at

FORT LARNED NATIONAL HISTORIC SITE, KANSAS

Fort Larned, Kansas, Hancock insisted on marching his command to their nearby village on Pawnee Fork so that, Custer wrote, it could "be seen by all the Indians." But Sand Creek was still fresh in the minds of the Cheyenne, and while their leaders delayed Hancock, the village was quickly abandoned. Hancock sent Custer after the fleeing Cheyenne, who split into small groups and struck out in different directions.

"I am of the opinion," Custer later wrote, "that no cavalry in the world, marching, even in the lightest manner possible . . . can overtake or outmarch the Western Indian, when the latter is disposed to prevent it." Custer did not know it, but one of his part-Indian interpreters was sympathetic to the people they were chasing and facilitated their escape. Nevertheless, Custer learned a significant lesson about Indian fighting—the soldiers had to catch them first.

Near Fort Hays, Kansas, Custer and his men came across the still-smoldering remains of a stage station and the bodies of its occupants. When Hancock received word of this attack, he ordered the abandoned village on Pawnee Fork burned to the ground. War had begun in earnest once again.

e᷎

WASHITA BATTLEFIELD NATIONAL HISTORIC SITE, OKLAHOMA

COURT-MARTIAL
AND REDEMPTION

*Custer, I rely on you in everything, and shall send you
on this expedition without orders, leaving you to act
entirely on your own judgment.*

PHILIP SHERIDAN, OCTOBER 4, 1868

During the early summer of 1867, Custer and six companies of
the Seventh marched through northwest Kansas, southwest
Nebraska, and northeast Colorado looking for warring Plains
bands, with little to show for their efforts. Custer parleyed twice
with Pawnee Killer, a Lakota chief, and naively accepted Pawnee
Killer's declarations of peace. This leader participated with his
warriors in the annihilation of a small military detachment led
by Lt. Lyman S. Kidder that July. Kidder's party of eleven men
was carrying dispatches meant for Custer. When Custer found

the hacked and disfigured remains of Kidder and his troopers, he described it as a sight that "even at this remote day makes my very blood curdle."

A noticeably moody Custer, undoubtedly frustrated by this very different mode of warfare, pushed his men and enforced shocking punishments. When one trooper forgot to water his horse at the proper time, Custer had a halter put around the man's neck and had him led to the creek where the horses were watered; this punishment was repeated more than once. Not surprisingly, soldiers deserted at every opportunity. One night, more than thirty men escaped into the darkness. The following afternoon, 13 men were seen deserting the regiment in broad daylight. Custer issued clear orders: Pursue and shoot the deserters. Three were wounded, one mortally. Custer publicly forbade the doctor from treating these men, although he discreetly gave the surgeon his consent that night. There were no more desertions.

By all accounts, Custer's thoughts during the campaign were absorbed with his wife, Libbie. His desire to be reunited with his young wife became so overwhelming that on July 15, 1867, he left most of his command at Fort Wallace and made a beeline for Fort Riley—without orders. Custer would later attempt to justify his forced march to Riley as a military necessity, but according to one of Libbie's letters, her husband knew he was risking a court-martial when he left Fort Wallace and "did it expecting the consequences." She added that "we are quite determined not to live apart again, even if he leaves the army." Custer was indeed placed under military arrest and charged with absence without leave, "conduct to the prejudice of good order and military discipline," and the unmerciful treatment of deserters. At a trial at Fort Leavenworth, Kansas, that fall, he was found guilty on all counts.

The sentence, announced officially on November 18, was suspension from rank and command, with loss of pay, for one year. The blow was softened considerably that winter by General Sheridan's offer to the Custers of the use of his personal quarters at Leavenworth. They accepted and spent the next few months enjoying the post's social scene.

Phil Sheridan had replaced General Hancock as the commander of the Department of the Missouri, so it now fell to him to answer the public cries to control the Plains tribes. As plans began in 1868 for an unprecedented winter campaign, he had only one individual in mind to command the main thrust of the expedition. On September 24, 1868, he sent a telegram to Custer: "Generals Sherman, Sully and myself, and nearly all the officers of your regiment, have asked for you. . . . Can you come at once? Eleven companies of your regiment will move about the 1st of October against the hostile Indians." Custer, his suspension lifted two months early, arrived at Fort Hays six days later.

The Seventh Cavalry would form part of a three-pronged movement aimed at the southern reaches of Indian Territory (present-day Oklahoma). "We are going to the heart of the Indian country," Custer wrote Libbie, "where white troops have never been before." Custer and the Seventh, along with companies of the Third U.S. Infantry, started south from Fort Dodge on November 12. After marching some 100 miles, the column halted near the junction of Beaver River and Wolf Creek, and set about establishing a supply depot for the coming operations, dubbed officially "Camp Supply." A few days later, on November 23, in the middle of a blinding snowstorm, Custer started his regiment on its mission to find the hostile camps. The regimental band, positioned at the head of the column, played "The Girl I Left Behind Me."

On November 26, a Thursday, Custer's Osage scouts discovered a fresh trail in the snow. Because there were no dog tracks, as would be found with a hunting party, the scouts were convinced it was the trail of a war party. Custer ordered immediate pursuit, the trail eventually leading them to the valley of the Washita River in the early-morning hours of November 27. A Cheyenne village lay sleeping in the valley. In the darkness, Custer heard a dog barking and the cry of a baby. Not wanting the inhabitants to slip out of his hands (like they had done with Hancock on Pawnee Fork) he divided his command of approximately 700 troopers into four battalions that would strike the village simultaneously from all sides. The attack would begin at first light with the band striking up "Garry Owen."

A shot rang out just before sunrise, and Custer made a quick signal for the band to begin playing. In a scene reminiscent of earlier days, the men with Custer burst into a loud cheer as their commander led them on a charge into the village, which they took completely by surprise. Custer, astride a black stallion, bounded across the river and into the camp, killing one Cheyenne with his pistol and riding down another. He continued to a prominent knoll overlooking the valley so as to better direct the fight. Warriors sold their lives dearly in the hopes of allowing their loved ones to escape, but to little avail. The battle for the village was over in a matter of minutes. When it was brought to Custer's attention that a group of women and children was being chased and shot, he ordered a stop to the bloodshed; fifty-three non-combatants were placed under guard in the village.

Unbeknownst to Custer when he planned his attack, there were a number of other villages downstream. Hundreds of warriors

WASHITA CAPTIVES

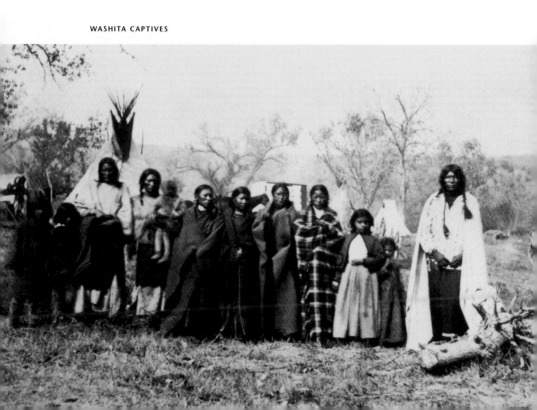

from these camps raced to the sound of the gunfire and began to taunt and threaten the cavalrymen as well as exchange a few shots. (The warriors were afraid to fire into the soldiers' midst for fear of hitting some of the captives.) Custer ordered the lodges burned and approximately 800 Indian ponies shot dead, afterward boasting to Sheridan that this group of Cheyenne "can neither fight, dress, sleep, eat or ride without sponging upon their friends."

Late that afternoon, while the band played "Ain't I Glad to Get Out of the Wilderness," he marched the Seventh and its Indian prisoners down the Washita in a feint that caused the opposing warriors to rush to the defense of their camps. As darkness fell, he swung his column around and returned upstream, eventually leaving the broad valley behind and setting a course for Camp Supply. Custer claimed in his official report that 103 Cheyenne were killed in the battle. Native accounts place the figure as low as twenty-nine men, women, and children.

The victory on the Washita secured Custer new fame as a successful Indian fighter, a reputation few men in the military could boast, but that fame did not come without controversy. First, the camp Custer attacked belonged to Black Kettle, a well-known peace proponent of the Southern Cheyenne whose village had been massacred at Sand Creek almost four years to the day earlier. The troopers killed Black Kettle and his wife at the Washita, which the Cheyenne and sympathizers maintained was another massacre. In Custer's defense, he did not know the identity of the village he was to attack, only that the trail led him to it.

A second controversy surrounded Custer's withdrawal from the battlefield without learning the fate of a small detachment under Maj. Joel Elliott, which had left the village area in pursuit of fleeing Cheyenne. Custer did make an attempt to find Elliott, but the growing number of warriors from the other villages forced him to consider the safety of the entire regiment. They learned later that Elliott and his detachment of seventeen had been surrounded and killed to a man. (These, along with Capt. Louis M. Hamilton, made up the total regimental dead in the engagement.)

℮⌐

PAPER BIRCH TREE IN
CUSTER STATE PARK, BLACK
HILLS, SOUTH DAKOTA

Yellowstone and Black Hills Expeditions

~

Custer is not belying his reputation—Which is that of a man selfishly indifferent to others, and ruthlessly determined to make himself conspicuous at all hazards.

2ND LT. CHARLES W. LARNED,
SEVENTH CAVALRY, APRIL 30, 1873

In the months following the Washita fight, Sheridan and Custer continued their pursuit of the free-roaming southern Plains people, coercing a portion of the Kiowa to move their lodges to Fort Cobb and freeing two white captives from the Cheyenne. When spring came, Sheridan offered Custer an indefinite leave in reward for his victory over Black Kettle. From a camp near Fort Hays, Custer and Libbie entertained a stream of countless visitors during the summer of 1869. Custer, a consummate sportsman

INTERIOR OF THE RECONSTRUCTED CUSTER HOME, FORT ABRAHAM LINCOLN STATE PARK, NORTH DAKOTA

hunted buffalo and other game, usually in the company of his guests. His most public sporting adventure occurred later as a member of the hunting party of the Grand Duke Alexis of Russia. Other members of the duke's celebrated hunt included Sheridan and Buffalo Bill Cody.

The early 1870s saw Custer again contemplating leaving the army. He devoted considerable time to various schemes designed to make him wealthy: a Colorado gold mine, Kansas real estate, railroad stock. His financial speculations on Wall Street and elsewhere were generally disasters. An exception was his agreement to write a series of articles on his Plains adventures for a popular magazine called *The Galaxy*. Each article brought him $100, and they were eventually gathered and published in book form in 1874 as *My Life on the Plains*. William Tecumseh Sherman, commanding general of the Army, informed Custer that his writings "on the Plains are by far the best I have ever read, and every member of my family has read the volume with deep interest."

From 1871 to 1873, Custer and the Seventh were stationed in Kentucky and other parts of the South on "Reconstruction duty." Custer, as he wrote Libbie, "preferred the plains." It must have come as a relief, then, when orders arrived in February 1873 directing Custer and the Seventh Cavalry to serve as an escort for an engineering party of the Northern Pacific Railroad that would be operating in the Yellowstone Basin of Montana Territory that summer. The railroad engineers would be traversing lands populated by bands of Lakota and Northern Cheyenne, who were decidedly opposed to any white men entering their country. Yet certain military men held strong beliefs that railroads were just what this region needed, and the Fort Laramie Treaty of 1868, as they knew, allowed such rail lines. "No one measure," Custer wrote, "so quickly and effectually frees a country from the horrors and devastations of Indian wars and Indian depredations generally as the building and successful operation of a railroad through the region overrun."

The Yellowstone Expedition started west from Fort Rice, Dakota Territory, on June 20. Under the overall command of Col. David S. Stanley, it consisted of ten companies of the Seventh Cavalry and nineteen companies of infantry, more than 1,400 soldiers. There were also the civilian engineers, scientists, and teamsters, totaling 353. One young officer commented on all the "English lords, scientists, and outsiders of every military description" accompanying the expedition, likening it to "a big picnic." It was no picnic, though, except perhaps in the eyes of Custer, who kept a careful tally of the game taken by his rifle, which included forty-one antelope.

As he had done in the past, Custer gathered around him what one cavalryman described as the "royal family," those officers, some of them family members, who were Custer supporters. Divisions within the regiment, which had begun during the Hancock Expedition of 1867 and widened after Washita and the Elliott affair, remained stronger than ever.

The Seventh had two sharp fights with the Lakota on the Yellowstone. On August 4, Custer with two companies (about ninety men) were surprised by some 300 Lakota but managed to hold them off for three hours until reinforcements arrived. A week later, having followed the trail to the Lakota's village, Custer with eight companies of the Seventh were attacked by what one trooper thought was "the whole Sioux Nation"—possibly as many as 1,000 warriors. The regimental band played "Garry Owen" as the troopers fired a volley into the oncoming warriors. After about twenty minutes, Custer ordered a charge, which caused the Plains fighters to flee. The troopers chased them for eight miles. Custer's thoroughbred bay gelding, King Bernadotte, was shot out from under him during the charge, but the Seventh had another victory.

The following September, the Seventh Cavalry returned to Fort Abraham Lincoln on the Missouri River, the regiment's new headquarters. After an uneventful winter, the Seventh embarked upon another large expedition this time into the heart of Lakota lands: the Black Hills of present-day South Dakota. On July 2, 1874, ten companies of the Seventh, two of infantry, more than 100 wagons, three Gatling guns, several scientists, newspaper reporters, and others began a march that would cover 883 miles when completed sixty days later. Custer's official mission was to scout possible locations for a new military post, but the expedition also included two miners who would settle once and for all persistent rumors of gold in the area.

Despite initial fears of hostile encounters similar to what the troopers had experienced on the Yellowstone the previous year, this expedition encountered no such opposition. Consequently, Custer hunted to his heart's content, writing to Libbie on August 15 that "I have reached the highest rung on the hunter's ladder of fame. I have killed my grizzly." But this news was nothing compared to what Custer had already sent to the outside world via a special courier: His miners had found gold.

e͡ɔ

REPLICA OF AN 1872 INFANTRY POST AT FORT ABRAHAM LINCOLN STATE PARK, NORTH DAKOTA

SITE OF THE INDIAN ENCAMPMENT ON THE
LITTLE BIGHORN RIVER, LITTLE BIGHORN
BATTLEFIELD NATIONAL MONUMENT, MONTANA

BATTLE OF
THE LITTLE BIGHORN

*If I were an Indian, I often think that I would
greatly prefer to cast my lot among those of my people
who adhered to the free open plains, rather than submit to
the confined limits of a reservation.*

GEORGE ARMSTRONG CUSTER, 1874

The discovery of gold in the Black Hills set in motion a series of
events that eventually led to the downfall of the Lakota and northern Cheyenne. Although the Treaty of 1868 forbade the presence
of white men on the Lakota reservation (except for military expe-
ditions), hundreds of miners streamed into the region. These
prospectors and town builders, as well as the residents of frontier
communities that profited as jumping off points for the goldfields,
demanded that the indigenous title to these lands be extinguished.
And that is exactly what the government set out to do in 1875. But

TATANKA-IYOTANKA (SITTING BULL), SPIRITUAL AND POLITICAL LEADER OF THE LAKOTA

negotiations to acquire the Black Hills failed, primarily because of the influence of Sitting Bull, Crazy Horse, and other powerful leaders. Non-agency Indians, or "hunting bands," who roamed the unceded Indian territory west of the Lakota reservation opposed all treaties or agreements with the white man, especially one that would sign away the Black Hills, which was a valuable hunting ground for them.

It became clear to U. S. Grant's administration, then, that the Black Hills could not be acquired without breaking the will of the hunting bands. Thus, in December 1875, runners were sent to the hunting bands with an order from the Indian Office requiring that they report to the reservation by January 31, 1876, or be "reported to the War Department as hostile Indians." But the hunting bands were not about to pull up and move their camps in the dead of winter. And as Wooden Leg, a Northern Cheyenne, later explained, "We were trying to stay away from all white people, and we wanted them to stay away from us." The deadline arrived and passed with no sign of the hunting bands, and the army began planning a military campaign that would commence in March 1876 in Montana Territory.

George Armstrong Custer was a big part of those plans, but he very nearly missed his date with destiny on the Little Bighorn. In April he testified before a congressional committee investigating claims of fraudulent activity by Secretary of War William W. Belknap, a Grant appointee. An angry President Grant responded by forbidding Custer from taking part in the summer's campaign. Only after Custer's pleadings and the intercession of his superiors (not to mention the bad press over the affair from anti-administration newspapers) did Grant finally relent. Custer and the Seventh, along with Custer's immediate superior, Brig. Gen. Alfred H. Terry, departed

Fort Lincoln on May 17. The twelve companies of the Seventh numbered thirty-three officers and 718 enlisted men. Custer's "royal family" this year included his brothers, Capt. Tom Custer and Boston Custer (forage master), nephew Autie Reed (named for his famous uncle), and brother-in-law Lt. James Calhoun.

The military columns reached the mouth of Rosebud Creek on the Yellowstone River in mid-June. Scouts discovered a trail south of the Yellowstone indicating that the expedition might find the hunting bands either on the Rosebud or on the next drainage to the west, the Little Bighorn River. Terry ordered Custer to take the Seventh and follow the trail, and to make sure that if it led him to the Little Bighorn, he should enter the valley far enough south of the supposed village to prevent the bands from escaping in that direction. Terry would go to the mouth of the Little Bighorn with a column under Col. John Gibbon and march upstream, thus trapping any Indians who were on the Little Bighorn between the two contingents. Custer and the Seventh set out at noon on the 22nd. He jotted a quick note to Libbie: "I hope to have a good report to send you by the next mail. A success will start us all toward [Fort] Lincoln."

Three days later, from a high prominence called the Crow's Nest, Custer and his Crow and Arikara scouts peered into the Little Bighorn Valley. The scouts assured him that a large village existed, but they also informed Custer that warriors roaming about the area had almost certainly discovered his column. In fact, troopers had that morning fired upon several Indians rummaging through a dropped pack on the column's back trail. These would soon carry the alarm to the village. This development changed everything for Custer. He had planned to conceal his command near the Crow's Nest for the remainder of the 25th, making a surprise attack on the morning of the 26th. But the element of surprise, so crucial to a successful campaign, was now rapidly slipping from his grasp. Fearing the Plains people would escape if he delayed longer, Custer ordered the Seventh to move out. After dropping into the valley, he divided his command into three battalions, sending one under Capt. Frederick W. Benteen in a southwesterly direction to scout for other possible camps. Maj. Marcus Reno, commanding another battalion, was to head toward the main village with Custer, who commanded the third battalion. The regiment's pack train with extra ammunition brought up the rear.

Upon approaching the village, Custer ordered Reno to ford the river and charge. Custer, now on the opposite side of the river, promised to support the major with "the whole outfit." As Reno advanced, Custer's column ascended the bluffs, where the general got his first good look at the huge village before him. It numbered approximately 1,000 lodges of the Lakota and Northern and Southern Cheyenne, home to some 7,000 men, women, and children. Custer now realized he would need the pack train with its ammunition and also Benteen's battalion. Consequently, he sent two separate couriers to retrieve them. The second of these, Trumpeter Giovanni Martini, carried hastily written orders: "Benteen. Come on. Big Village. Be Quick. Bring Packs. W. W. Cooke. P. S. bring pacs." Those were the last words from Custer and his men.

Major Reno, alarmed at the number of Lakota and Cheyenne massing in his front, halted his charge just short of the village. He was subsequently forced to retreat first to some timber near the river and then to the bluff tops on the other side, taking heavy casualties along the way. When Benteen, who was marching to Custer, encountered Major Reno and his demoralized battalion, Reno asked Benteen to halt his command and reinforce the major's position. As for Custer's movements, in the words of biographer Frederic F. Van de Water, "No one will ever completely know his purpose or learn the instant and manner of his death."

Van de Water wrote this in 1934, but even today, with additional evidence from battlefield archeology and a reexamination of the many Indian accounts of the fight, many questions are left unanswered. Abundant theories concerning how Custer's "Last Stand" evolved have appeared in books, newspapers, magazines, and films, yet it remains the ultimate historical enigma. The one thing that is certain, though, is that the Lakota and Cheyenne, defending their families and homes, destroyed Custer and the 210 troopers of his battalion that day on the long ridges overlooking the Little Bighorn.

The Terry and Gibbon column arrived at the battlefield on June 27, from the north, after the large village had decamped. They found Reno and Benteen's exhausted command on what would become known as Reno Hill; they had lost 53 men killed. For the first time, Reno and Benteen's men learned the shocking news of Custer and his troopers' death, whose bodies Gibbon's scouts had discovered four miles to the north. The bodies of their comrades had been stripped and mutilated by the victorious Lakota and Cheyenne. On Custer's body were discovered two bullet wounds, one in the temple and one in the left breast. Before the troopers buried him, someone clipped a lock of his hair for Libbie. Custer's remains were exhumed a year later and transferred to West Point.

Ironically, Custer's sensational defeat guaranteed the quick demise of the roving hunting bands and the loss of their beloved Black Hills, for an outraged nation demanded swift retaliation. The army had driven all the Plains people onto reservations within a few short years.

Libbie Custer never remarried, instead making it her life's work to guard and honor the memory of her husband. She died in 1933 and now lies next to Custer. Among the numerous papers she left behind was a letter of condolence written by George B. McClellan, Custer's old Civil War commander. "It is some consolation to me," he wrote, "I cannot doubt it is to you—that he died as he had lived, a gallant gentleman, a true hero, fighting unflinchingly to the last against desperate odds. His death was as he would have had it, with his face to the foe, encouraging his men to the last." It is that iconic image of George Armstrong Custer, whether accurate or not, that remains the most conspicuous in the American consciousness.

Custer, Elizabeth Bacon. *Boots and Saddles*. New York: Harper & Brothers, 1885.

Custer, George A. *My Life on the Plains*. New York: Sheldon & Co., 1874.

Hutton, Paul, ed. *The Custer Reader*. Lincoln: University of Nebraska Press, 1992.

Katz, D. Mark. *Custer in Photographs*. New York: Bonanza Books, 1990.

Sklenar, Larry. *To Hell with Honor: Custer and the Little Bighorn*. Norman: University of Oklahoma Press, 2000.

Urwin, Gregory J. W. *Custer Victorious: The Civil War Battles of General George Armstrong Custer*. Edison, N.J.: Blue & Grey Press, 1983.

Utley, Robert M. *Cavalier in Buckskin: George Armstrong Custer and the Western Military Frontier*. Revised edition. Norman: University of Oklahoma Press, 2001.

Wert, Jeffry D. *Custer: The Controversial Life of George Armstrong Custer*. New York: Simon & Schuster, 1996.

Whittaker, Frederick. *A Complete Life of General George A. Custer*. New York: Sheldon & Co., 1876.